Just Duct Tape It!

LEISURE ARTS, INC.
Little Rock, Arkansas

Table of Contents

EDITORIAL STAFF
Vice President and Editor-in-Chief: Susan White Sullivan
Craft Publications Director: Cheryl Johnson
Special Projects Director: Susan Frantz Wiles
Senior Prepress Director: Mark Hawkins
Art Publications Director: Rhonda Shelby
Special Projects Designer: Patti Wallenfang
Technical Writer: Mary Sullivan Hutcheson
Editorial Writer: Susan McManus Johnson
Art Category Manager: Lora Puls
Senior Publications Designer: Dana Vaughn
Graphic Artists: Dayle Carroza and Kara Darling
Imaging Technician: Stephanie Johnson
Prepress Technician: Janie Marie Wright
Photography Manager: Katherine Laughlin
Contributing Photographer: Ken West
Contributing Photo Stylists: Sondra Daniel and Brooke Duszota
Publishing Systems Administrator: Becky Riddle
Mac Information Technology Specialist: Robert Young

BUSINESS STAFF
President and Chief Executive Officer: Rick Barton
Vice President of Sales: Mike Behar
Director of Finance and Administration: Laticia Mull Dittrich
National Sales Director: Martha Adams
Creative Services: Chaska Lucas
Information Technology Director: Hermine Linz
Controller: Francis Caple
Vice President, Operations: Jim Dittrich
Retail Customer Service Manager: Stan Raynor
Print Production Manager: Fred F. Pruss

ISBN-13: 978-1-46470-155-9

Just Duct Tape It!

Here's a fantastic idea that's really sticking around—creating with duct tape! You'll find it in dozens of colors and prints, but it's not just another pretty tape! Duct tape is still strong enough to hang tough, so why not make it into original handbags and wallets? You can fashion a bouquet of wild flowers or a bright bangle bracelet. Headed to school? Make magnetic wallpaper and matching accessories for the best-looking locker, ever! Your friends will be amazed at your creative ways!

Basics

duct tape hints

Working with duct tape is quick & easy! Here are a few tips we picked up while building these projects, but there are endless options. Get creative & have fun!

- Scissors work for cutting small pieces of tape & clipping curves.
- It's super quick to use a craft knife & metal ruler when cutting strips & sheets. Craft knives are sharp & safety is important.
- A self-healing cutting mat protects the table & has lots of guidelines for measuring & aligning the tape strips. To remove the tape from the mat, use the tip of the knife blade to pick up a corner of the tape.
- Once you've stuck 2 pieces of tape together, smooth your finger or hand over the overlapped areas to make sure they really stick.

making a single-sided sheet

Stick the duct tape end to the cutting mat & roll out to the indicated measurement. Cut the strip from the roll.

cut

Stick a second strip to the mat, overlapping the first strip by about $1/4$". Continue adding strips until you have the size sheet you need.

$1/4$" overlap [

Cut the strips a bit longer than called for; then, trim the sheet to size.

making a double-sided sheet

Follow the instructions for Making a Single-Sided Sheet (page 5) to make 2 sheets. Remove the sheets from the cutting mat & stick to each other.

smooth ←

Cut the strips a bit longer than called for. After sticking both sheets together, trim to size.

making a double-sided strip

Cut 2 strips of tape & stick to each other.

← smooth →

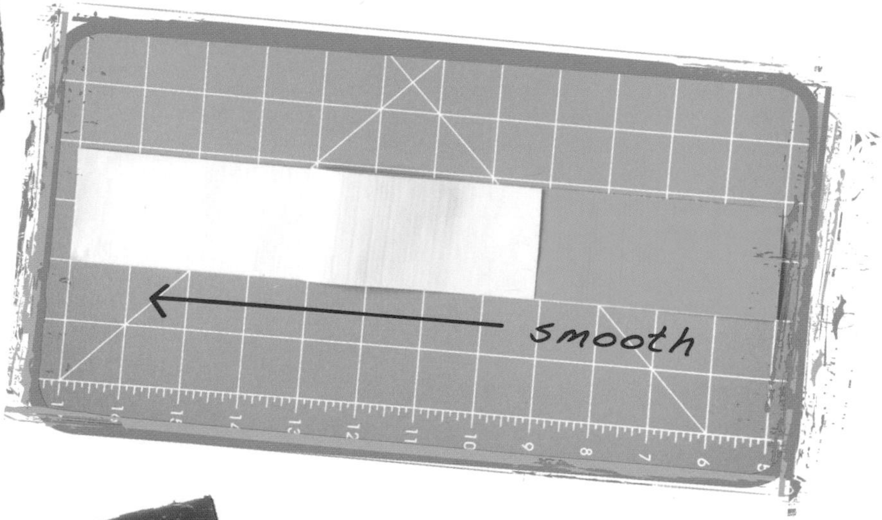

making an offset strip

Cut 2 strips of tape & stick to each other, offsetting the top strip by about $3/8$". One sticky edge is usually trimmed off.

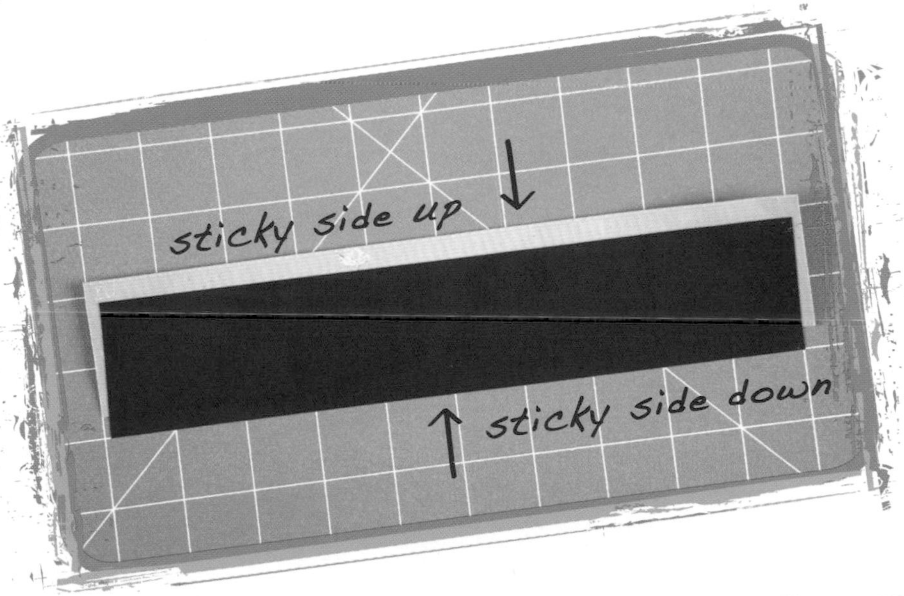

sticky side up ↓

↑ sticky side down

covering an edge

Cut the tape a bit longer than the edge to be covered; trim to the desired width. The projects typically use $1/2"$, $1"$, $1^{1}/_{2}"$, and the whole tape width. Place the edge about halfway over the strip; fold the strip down to cover the edge.

fold & stick

making a strap

Cut a strip the indicated length. Trim the width (see below). Place the tape, sticky side up, on the cutting mat. Fold one long edge about $1/3$ of the way toward the middle.

fold about $1/3$ up

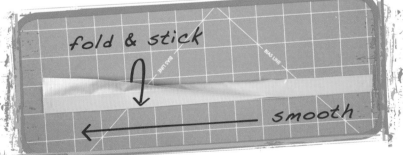

fold & stick

smooth

Fold down the other long edge & smooth.

The strips are 3x the width of the finished strap. So,
$3/4"$ strip = $1/4"$ wide strap
$1^{1}/_{2}"$w strip = $1/2"$ wide strap
$2^{1}/_{4}"$w pieced strip = $3/4"$ wide strap
$3"$w pieced strip = $1"$ wide strap

Covered button kits come with 2 pieces.

Stick tape to the domed side of the button. Clip the curves & wrap the tape to the inside of the button.

Push the button bottom into the button.

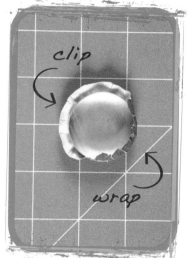

clip

wrap

making covered string

Cut a tape strip & lay a piece of string along the edge. Tightly roll until the string is covered. Trim the excess tape.

roll & trim excess

Materials: duct tape (green & assorted colors & prints); straws; empty water bottle; dried beans

Flower & Leaf: Make an offset strip (page 7) for petals. Make another 1 in a different color for the fringed center.

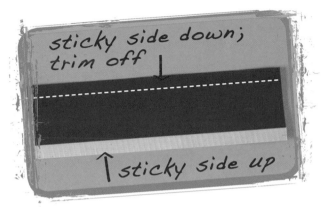

sticky side down; trim off

sticky side up

Make a double-sided green strip (page 7) for the leaves. Freehand cut the petals & leaves.

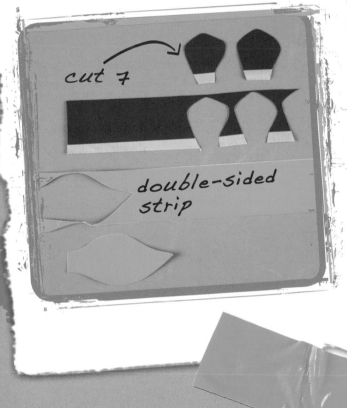

cut 7

double-sided strip

Wrap 2 straws with green tape.

roll

1" wide strip

Wrap & tape the fringed center around the straw.

Cut fringe 1st!

Continued on page 12.

Wild Flowers

Wild Flowers
continued

Vase: Cut the top off the water bottle. Decorate with strips of tape. Place a handful of beans in the vase bottom. Add the flowers & leaves.

Tape the petals & leaf to the straws.

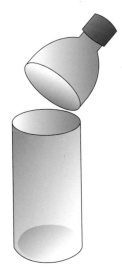

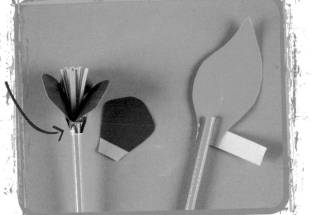

wrap with green tape

Bonus

For a cute pen, tape the fringed center & petals to an ink pen. Wrap with a bit of ribbon & finish off with a wrap of pink zebra.

Materials: used duct tape rolls with a bit left on the roll; duct tape (coordinating colors); lamp with shade

End of the Roll Lamp

Stick the rolls together. Trim the shade. Place rolls over the lamp base.

trim to ³/₄" wide

¹/₄"w strip

cover the top edge (page 8)

13

Walk
on the
Wild Side

Table

Materials: duct tape (2 animal prints & chrome); assemble-it-yourself 20" square side table

Put the table together. Make two 17" square single-sided sheets (page 5) & cut $3^7/_8$" squares.

Stick the squares to the table top. Cover the table sides with chrome tape.

Tagging Along Luggage Tags

Materials: duct tape (2 coordinating colors or prints); clear plastic badge holder; adhesive-backed hook & loop fastener

Insert the photo or name tag into the badge holder. Cover the edges with tape (page 8).

Make a $1/2$" x 7" strap (page 8). Cut a slit in the center & insert the strap.

Hailey Smith
5701 Ranch Dr.
Hazen, Texas

naked badge holder

trim to points →

hook & loop fastener

Materials: duct tape; 7/8"w ribbon (your waist measurement + 36")

Ribbon Belts

Cut a tape strip your waist measurement. Center & fold the tape over the ribbon edges.

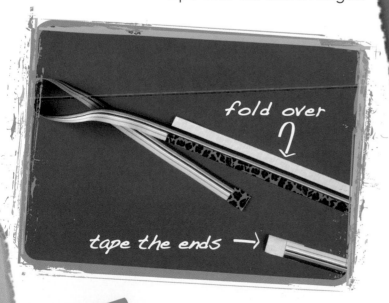

fold over

tape the ends →

Make a double-sided tape strip (page 7). Add a narrower coordinating strip down the middle of the bracelet.

Cover a 1½" long string (page 9). Attach the button. Add the hook & loop fasteners to the bracelet ends.

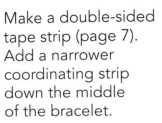

wrist + 1½"

double-sided strip

trim to 1½" or leave wide

punch holes   covered string

tape the string ends down

Big Flower Bracelets

Materials: duct tape (2 coordinating colors or prints); string; big flower button; ⅛" hole punch; self-adhesive hook & loop fasteners

Cuff Bracelets

Materials: duct tape (3-4 coordinating colors or prints); self-adhesive jeweled flowers; string; $1/8$" hole punch; $1^1/2$" covered-button kit; self-adhesive hook & loop fasteners

Make a double-sided $2^1/2$" wide sheet (page 6) that is $1^1/2$" longer than your wrist and embellish.

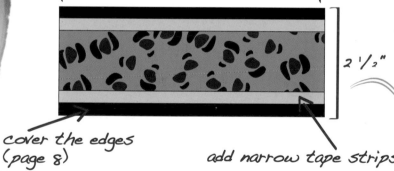

wrist + $1^1/2$"

$2^1/2$"

cover the edges (page 8)

add narrow tape strips

For the jeweled flower bracelet, add 3 flowers to the bracelet center. Add the hook & loop fasteners to the bracelet ends.

For the buttoned bracelet, cover the button (page 9) & add a jeweled flower.

Cover a $1^1/2$" long string (page 9). Attach the button (see drawing, opposite). Add the hook & loop fasteners to the bracelet ends.

Materials: duct tape; chenille stem; bead-style charms

Twist on the Wrist Bracelet

Cut a tape strip that is 6" longer than the chenille stem & cover the chenille stem.

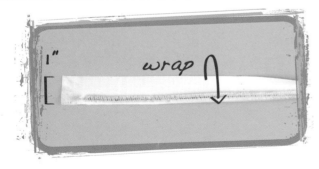

1"

wrap

Flatten & trim the bracelet ends; slide on charms. Knot the bracelet ends.

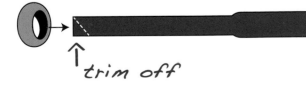

trim off

Blinged-Out Bracelets

Materials: duct tape (2 coordinating colors or prints); blingy decoration – shank-style buttons or a self-adhesive jewel patch; self-adhesive hook & loop fasteners

For the single button bracelet, cover a 1½" long string (page 9). Attach the button. Or make 3 strings & attach 3 buttons! Add the hook & loop fasteners to the bracelet ends.

Make a double-sided sheet (page 6), trim to the desired width, & embellish.

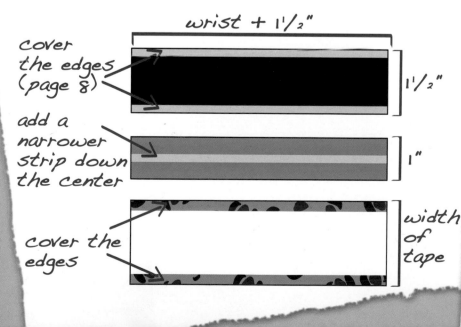

wrist + 1½"

cover the edges (page 8)

1½"

add a narrower strip down the center

1"

cover the edges

width of tape

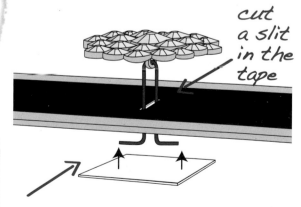

cut a slit in the tape

tape the string ends down

For the jeweled bracelet, add the patch to the bracelet. Add the hook & loop fasteners to the bracelet ends.

21

Fun Flip-Flops

Materials: duct tape (2 coordinating colors or prints); cardboard; buttons & 1/8" hole punch (optional)

Draw around your favorite pair of shoes or flip-flops on the cardboard & cut out.

Place flip-flops on a single-sided sheet of tape (page 5).

Cut out & wrap the tape to the back of each shape.

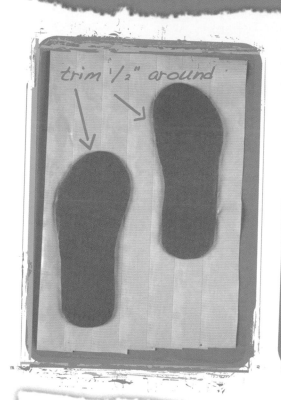

trim 1/2" around

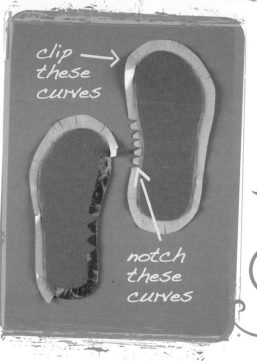

clip → these curves

notch these curves

Mark between your toes and cut a slit above the mark.

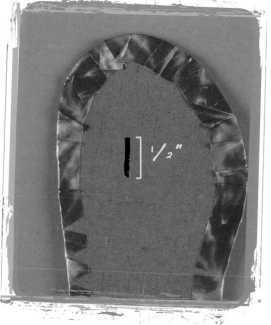

1/2"

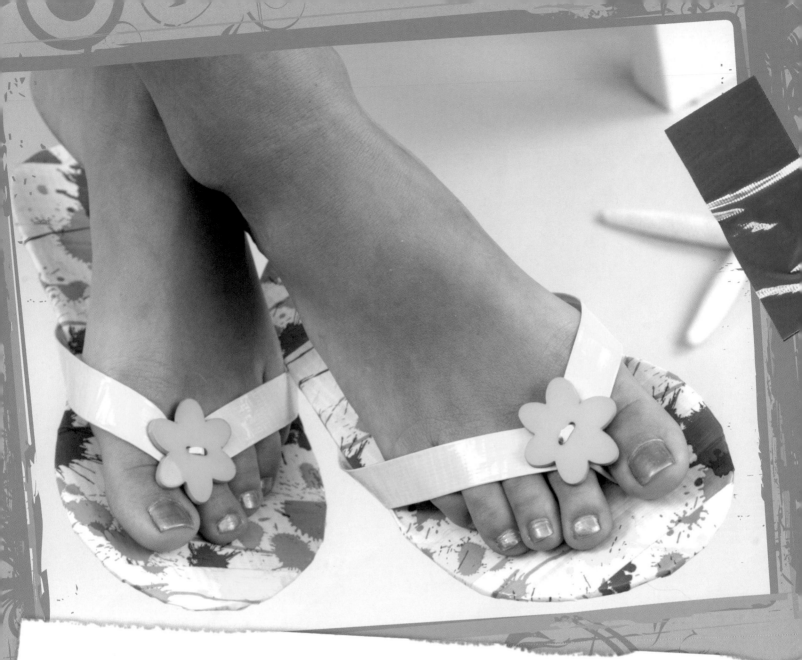

Make a ½" x 24" strap (page 8). Fold in half & slide it through the slit.

1"

tape down

Cut a half width of tape; wrap it around the strap.

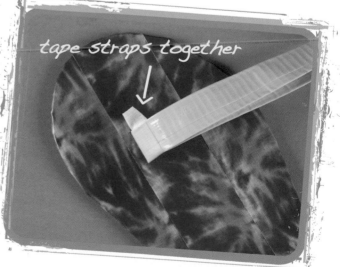

tape straps together

Continued on page 24.

Fun Flip-Flops
continued

Tape the straps to the bottom & trim.

Make a covered string (page 9) & add a button if you'd like (see drawing on page 18 for more info).

Cover each flip-flop bottom with tape.

tape here & here

trim

Kozy Koozies

Materials: duct tape (3 coordinating colors or prints); 8" x 3" felt piece; self-adhesive hook & loop fastener strip

Trim a straw with tape

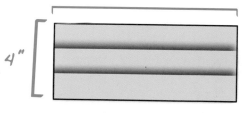

Make 2 single-sided sheets (page 5). Sandwich the felt & the sheets.

Cover the edges (page 8) & add the fastener.

10"

4"

4"

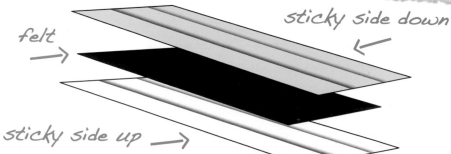

sticky side down

felt →

sticky side up →

25

Materials: duct tape (2 coordinating colors); ⅛" wide ribbon; scallop-edged scissors; self-adhesive foam letters; paint pen

Mini Banner

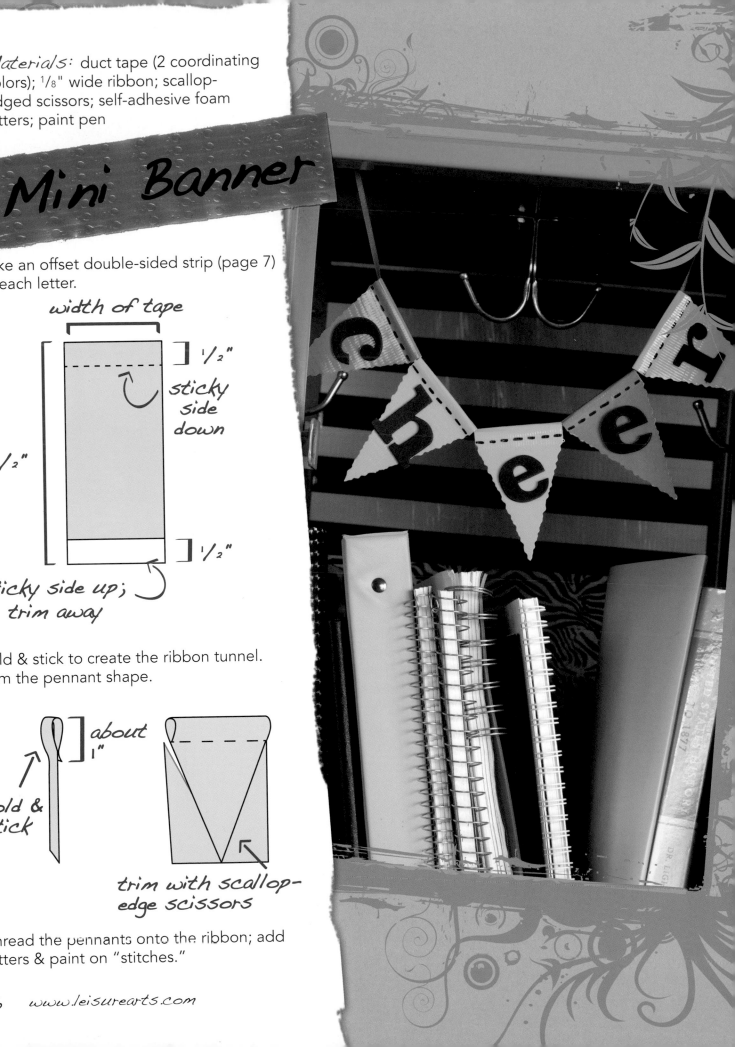

Make an offset double-sided strip (page 7) for each letter.

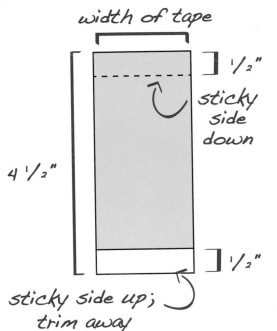

width of tape

½"

sticky side down

4½"

½"

sticky side up; trim away

Fold & stick to create the ribbon tunnel. Trim the pennant shape.

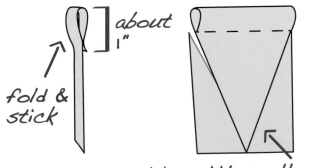

about 1"

fold & stick

trim with scallop-edge scissors

Thread the pennants onto the ribbon; add letters & paint on "stitches."

27

Materials: duct tape (coordinating colors); chenille stem; scallop-edged scissors; self-adhesive magnetic discs & sheets; 1⅛" covered button kit; self-adhesive jewels; paint pens

Magnets

Smile: Make a double-sided strip (page 7). Cut a scalloped oval, decorate, & add the magnetic sheet.

Button: Cover a button with tape (page 9). Add a bit of bling & a magnetic disc.

Personalized: Make a 5½" x 3" multi-colored, double-sided sheet (page 6). Trim the corners & add a trimmed black center. Add the magnetic sheet & a jeweled flower; personalize with the paint pen.

Flower: Make a double-sided strip (page 7) & cut petals.

cut 7 petals

Cover the chenille stem & twist.

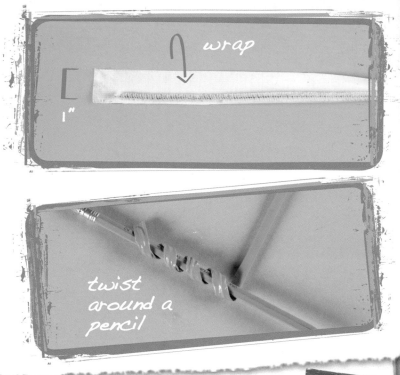

wrap

1"

twist around a pencil

Cover a button with tape (page 9). Cover a 1½" string (page 9). Arrange & tape the petals together. Attach the button. Add the magnetic disc and twisted stem.

tape petals together

tape down & add magnet

thread string through button

Trim the ends off the craft sticks.

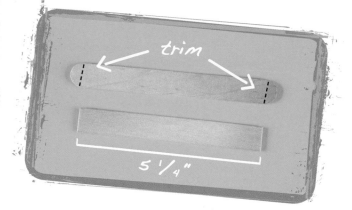

trim

5 ¹/₄"

Make a multi-colored single-sided sheet (page 5). Cut the sheet & cover the sticks.

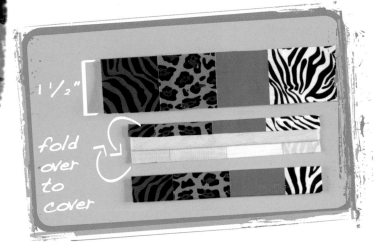

1 ¹/₂"

fold over to cover

Tape the frame together. Tape the photo to the frame back. Add the magnets & hearts to the frame.

overlap sticks & tape together

Frame

Materials: duct tape (4 coordinating colors & prints); self-adhesive jeweled hearts; 4 craft sticks; 4 ³/₄" self-adhesive magnets

Materials: duct tape (4 coordinating colors & prints); magnetic locker mirror; self-adhesive jeweled flowers; self-adhesive magnetic sheet

Mirror

2 1/2" larger than mirror

Make a multi-colored double-sided sheet (page 6) & cut out the middle.

4 1/2"

6"

2 1/2" larger than mirror

Tape the sheet to the mirror back & add magnets.

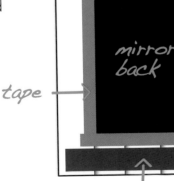

mirror back

tape

magnet

Add the flowers to the mirror.

Science Project Due Friday!

Pencil Cup

Materials: duct tape (4 coordinating colors & prints); magnetic pencil cup; self-adhesive jeweled flower

Make several offset double-sided strips of tape (page 7) & fringe.

Make a 1/2" x 10" strap (page 8).

Stick the fringe to the cup. Tape the strap to the cup. Add the flower.

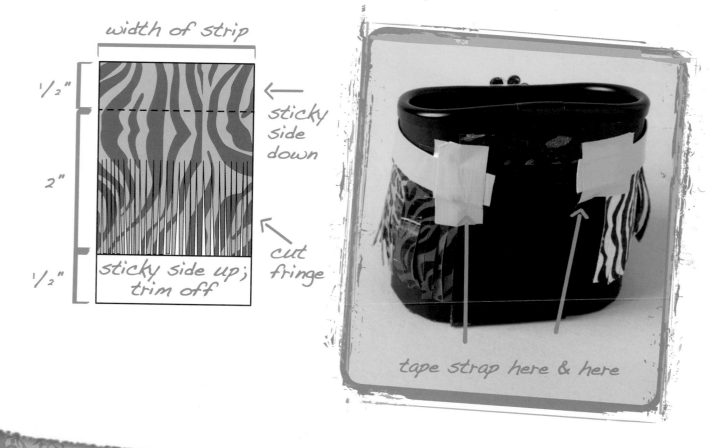

width of strip

1/2"

2"

1/2"

sticky side down

cut fringe

sticky side up; trim off

tape strap here & here

Materials: duct tape; magnetic sheet

Our wallpaper sheets are about 8" x 11" each.

Wallpaper

Make double-sided sheets (page 6) to fit the locker.

Add magnetic strips to the backs.

Peace, Love & Ribbon Bag

Materials: duct tape (tan, brown, white, & leopard); 7/8" & 1/8" wide ribbon; peace pendant; string; self-adhesive glittery chipboard letter; 1/4" hole punch

Finished Size: 8"w x 9¼"h with a 7" flap

Bag: Make an 8" x 25½" double-sided sheet (page 6), with tan on both sides. Fold the sheet & tape the sides together. Cover all the edges (page 8) with a half width of brown tape.

16 ½"

9"

tape these edges together with tan

Make a 1" x 38" strap (page 8) & tape to the bag back.

tape down

Continued on page 34.

Peace, Love & Ribbon

Bag continued

Tag: Make a double-sided brown strip (page 7) & embellish it with tan & leopard. Cover a 9" string with brown (page 9). Loop the string through the tag; tie the tag & the pendant to the bag.

Trim the flap with ribbon & tape.

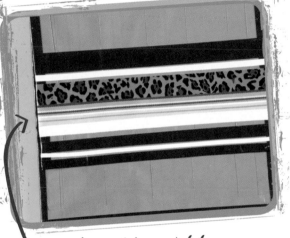

overlap the ribbon with tape

personalize with some bling!

tie on with ribbon

Circles
Squared
Tote Bag

Materials: duct tape (camo, leopard, & black – 1 roll each; small amounts of pink zebra, paint splat, chrome, pink tie dye, black/white checkerboard, & zebra); four 1" D-rings; two 27" lengths of ⅝" diameter rope; fob-style key ring; bead-style charms; charm holder; 10" x 4" piece of sturdy cardboard; stapler

Finished Size: 12"w x 14"d

Bag: Make a 33" x 15" double-sided sheet (page 6), with camo on 1 side & leopard on the other. Fold the sheet; staple the sides together. Cover the stapled edges (page 8) with black tape.

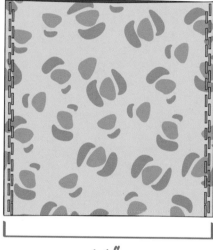

16 ½"

15"

Flatten each bottom corner to form a point. Staple across each corner. Turn the bag right side out.

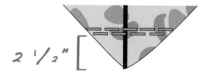

2 ½"

Cover the top edge with black tape. Completely cover the cardboard with leopard tape & insert into the bag.

Handle Tabs: Make four 1" x 6" straps (page 8). Thread the ends through the D-rings . Use black to tape the tab ends to the bag. Add another strip of black tape to the inside top edge.

tape down one end

tape down other end

add more tape

Continued on page 38.

Circles Squared Tote Bag *continued*

Handles: Wrap each rope with leopard tape & attach to the D-rings.

1 1/2"

roll & trim excess

wrap with black & chrome

Circles: Make single-sided sheets (page 5) of printed tapes & one of black tape. Cut out & stick print circles to the black sheet. Add the circles to the bag front.

traced inside of roll

trim 1/4" away

Tassel: Make a double-sided sheet of pink zebra tape & fringe. Make a 1/4" x 7" strap of leopard tape. Thread the strap through the key ring & tape to the fringed sheet. Roll & wrap the fringed sheet; add the charms.

10"

1"

6"

roll

wrap with chrome & black

Do the Ruffle Bag

Materials: duct tape (purple, leopard, & black); string; chain for handle

Finished Size: 6" x 7½"

Ruffles: Make two 12" off-set strips (page 7). Fold each strip to create a string tunnel.

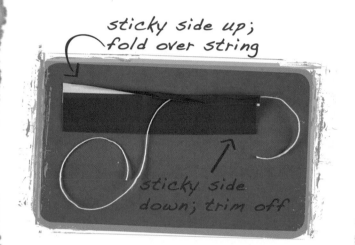

sticky side up; fold over string

sticky side down; trim off

Gather each ruffle.

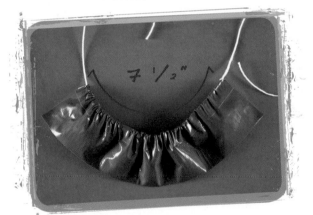

7 ½"

Leopard Band: Make a 19" double-sided leopard strip (page 7). Cover the edges with black (page 8).

Bag: Make a 6" x 15" double-sided sheet (page 6), with purple on both sides. Fold the sheet; use purple tape to join the sides. Cover the top edge with purple.

Tape the ruffles to the bag.

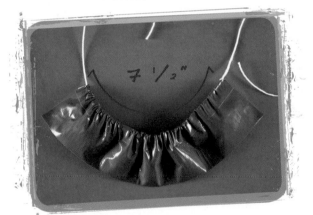

tape ruffles to bag

Continued on page 42.

Wrap the leopard band around the bag & tape inside.

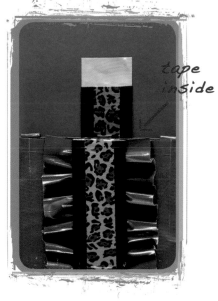

Handle Tabs: Make two 1" x 4" straps; cover two 4" long string pieces (page 9). Thread the string through the chain ends & tape the string ends together.

Thread the tab ends through string rings. Tape the tab ends to the bag.

Do the Ruffle Bag
continued

Maxed Out Clutch

Materials: duct tape (4-5 colors or prints); hook & loop fastener

Finished Size: 7$\frac{1}{2}$" x 4$\frac{1}{4}$" folded

This clutch is great in so many colors—we went wild with yellow, aqua, zebra, and leopard, too!

Continued on page 44.

Maxed Out Clutch

continued

Make a 7½" x 11½" double-sided sheet (page 6), with 2 colors of tape. Cover the edges (page 8) with a third tape.

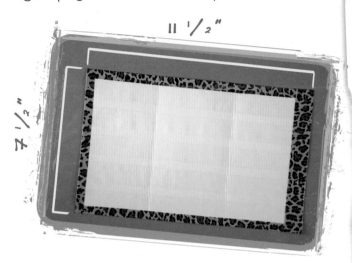

11 ½"

7 ½"

Card Pockets: Make a 20" double-sided tape strip (page 7). Cut 6 pockets & cover the edges.

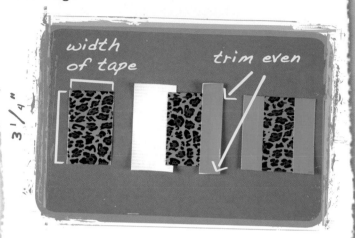

width of tape

trim even

3 ¼"

Bill Holder: Make a 7¼" x 3" double-sided sheet; tape to the clutch inside.

tape

leave open

tape

tape

Tape the pockets together.

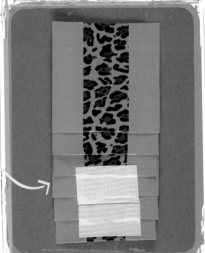

tape each pocket separately

For more style, add tape strips to trim this section and the front. You can't have enough tape!

Tape the pockets in place.

tape

tape

tape

Fold the clutch in thirds & add the hook & loop fastener.

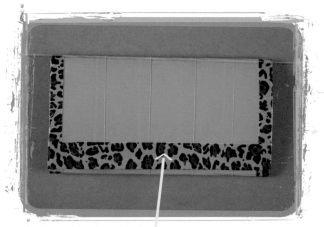

add the fastener inside

Materials: duct tape (3-5 colors or prints); plastic badge holder

Finished Size: 4¼" x 3¼" folded

Dude, Where's My Wallet?

Make a 8½" x 7" double-sided sheet (page 6), with the same color on each side & stripes on the front. Fold the sheet; tape the sides together.

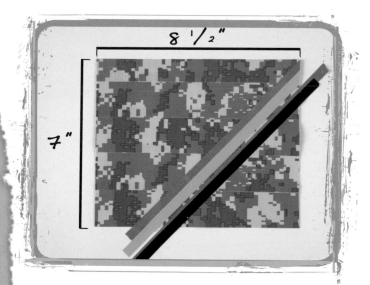

8 ½"

7"

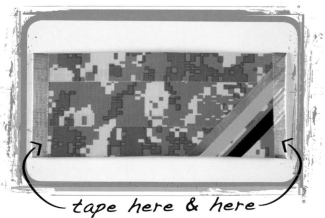

tape here & here

Add the clear badge holder.

single layer of plastic

trim even

tape

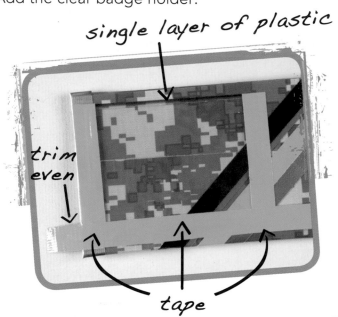

Make a 15" double-sided tape strip (page 7). Cover the top edge (page 8) & cut 4 pockets.

cover the edges

$3 \ ^3/_4$"

cut 4 pockets

Stack the pockets & tape to the wallet. Fold in half.

tape

tape

tape

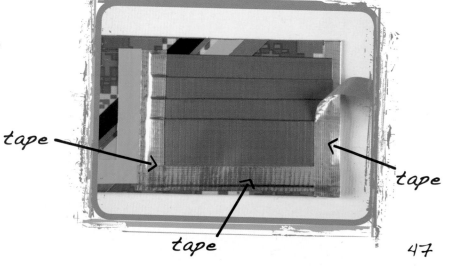

Tape Info

Each project in this leaflet was made using ShurTech Brands' Duck Tape® brand duct tape. For your convenience, listed below are the specific tapes used to create the photography models.

Colors
Electric Blue™
Atomic Yellow® X-Factor™
Cookie Dough™
Midnight Madness™
Blaze Orange® X-Factor™
Mud Puddle™
Chrome® X-Factor™
Funky Flamingo® X-Factor™
Island Lime® X-Factor™
Purple Duchess™
Winking White™

Prints
Cosmic Tie-Dye™
Digital Camo
Hardwood Camouflage
Hot Rod™
Paint Splatter
Pink Zebra
Spotted Leopard™
Totally Tie-Dye™
Zig-Zag Zebra™